DEPARTING FLIGHTS AND ENDLESS NIGHTS

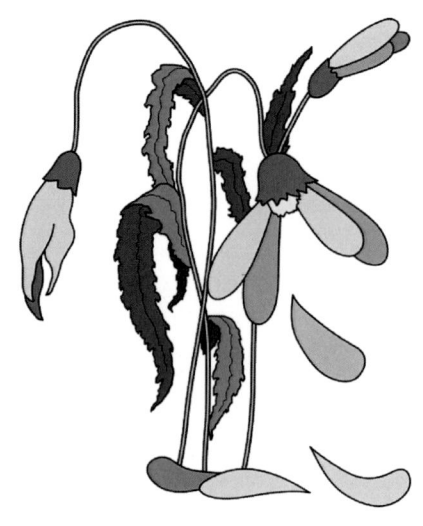

My intention
with *Departing Flights and Endless Nights* has
always been to write past the fear of exposure.
The poems on these pages represent the raw
emotions of a young woman trying to live a
balanced life while working in the music industry.
They were written on the go from the passenger
seat of a van to various hotel hallways and parking
lots throughout the country. I've included some of
my favorite photographs shot on film throughout
the years to showcase some of my favorite
memories. I found my voice through traveling and
I am forever grateful for that.
- Britt

different city, same routine

i woke up to the sound of pouring rain today.
the thought of leaving my tiny coffin
didn't even cross my mind.

another hotel lobby
full of ghosts.

four quarters in the washing machine
and four walls that feel familiar.

different city, same routine.

700 club

liquor lips and desperate for attention;
i hate myself when i get like this.

cloudy eyed uber ride
taking me to a destination unknown.

i've learned tonight
that i should no longer try
to fill this hole in my soul
with tainted waters.

flowers won't be able to bloom there.

daze off

i climbed massive red rocks
in moab, utah yesterday.

i crushed insecurities
step by step
over coral colored boulders,
smooth as silk.

how could something
from the earth
be so heavy
yet feel so delicate
to the touch?

my softness is revealed
as i look down
at the palm of my hands.
they are not made of stone.

my landscape radiates gold,
even on the darkest of days.

my head is weightless
like the pink clouds gazing back at me.

i will no longer allow anyone
to tell me that
my brittle body
is too heavy.

running out of gas

i can still picture the way
you turned and looked at me
as the van puttered to a halt.

now stuck on the side of a highway
in the middle of nowhere
laughing under covers.

for hours we took turns driving
and singing our favorite songs.
everyone else got some restless sleep.

all that smiling and star gazing,
we simply forgot to fill up the tank.

Locations: Michigan, Minnesota and Québec. On tour with: Hammerfall, Hoodie Allen and Polyphia.

nashville

i see you walk towards me
in my peripheral vision.
you blew right past me,
a whirlwind of destruction.

the warm air moves upward.
the area around me becomes cold.
we lock eyes for a moment,
now the storm is going to unfold.

there is a girl behind you,
she's tugging on your vest.
i truly wish i could warn her
that tornadoes will leave
an aching pain in the chest.

montana

waking up
while the bus is still moving;
a true delight.
i'm greeted by the sun
and the clanking sound of
beer bottles swaying in the fridge.
i decide to pop in my headphones
and take a seat at the marble table.
this is where I enjoy sitting
on every bus i've ever lived in.
it's the little joys on tour that matter,
such as facing forward
and looking out of the windows.
enjoying the quiet, if only for a moment,
becomes very important.
the table gives me a sense of security,
a stillness,
or perhaps just a stable surface
to place my hot coffee in between sips.
this is my time,
before the sleeping souls
in the dark alley wake.
when they wake, a new day has begun.

summer's end

i shut my trailer door for the last time
and then went to lay down on another.
i could have left by now, but I needed to stay.
drenched in summer rain and sunscreen,
i look to my new australian friends for comfort.
"we're are all just a bunch of crumbs
cut from the same loaf." says eaven,
while holding a bottle of scotch.
there's another guy sitting in a cardboard box laughing.
chucky started throwing leftover coolers,
merch bins and dolly's into a trash pile.
elisha is taking photos and i am in tears.

this was the hardest summer of my life,
yet i'm so sad to see it end.
the storms, the broken generators,
the trailers detaching from the bus
in the middle of the night,
the 20 show stretch,
the mental breakdowns; all of it was worth it.

i feel like I made an impact this summer.
i brought women together
and made so many new friends.
the number one traveling circus
has finally come to a bittersweet end.

goodbyes

"thanks for being the light of this tour."
that has got to be
one of the nicest goodbyes
that i have ever received.

i shut the bus door behind me
for the very last time
and walked into the airport
with the rest of my crew.
i hear a little boy yell
"look mommy, they must be rock stars!"
we turned and smiled,
then proceeded to walk to the kiosk.

if only that little boy knew
we were flying on spirit.

Locations: Georgia, Massachusetts, Texas and Vancouver. On tour with: Flotsam and Jetsam, Hammerfall and Rainbow Kitten Surprise

knock gently

i am persistent.

i find myself constantly knocking on doors that aren't meant
to open for me. if there's a sign that says "do not enter" i am
more eager to open up that creaky gate and walk right up
onto the front porch. i will peak into the living room
window and knock on the door until my knuckles bleed.

but I won't do that with you.

i finally see a house with a sign that says "welcome" in
bright yellow. there's beautiful ivy crawling up the brick
walls and laughter coming from the inside. the red door
looks so inviting but i will not knock. i will not knock.

you see, something I've learned recently is that you can not
rush a good thing. we force the wrong people into our lives
so quickly because we feel that we can change them; mold
them into the perfect shape. you know, the kind of shape
that is missing from our souls. we are trying to fill our bellies
with anything that will make us feel whole again, even if
that means sitting at a dinner table full of food we hate
across from a man that makes us feel like we are less of a
woman. we all have to eat.

so when you stumble along someone good,
don't rush it. you have to let it flow. they are just being
cautious, protecting their home, their heart.

so be patient with the broken.
allow them to invite you in.
do not bang that door down.

if anything, knock gently.

pardon me!

you could have
had all of me.
you may think that
you're not good enough,
but you just chose
not to be.
pardon me,
for thinking that
you could have been
something special.

polyphia

it's hard to believe that 6 weeks ago
these beautiful souls were strangers.

i'm currently sitting in the van,
with bags at my feet,
and hotel coffee in the cup holder.
water bottles full of piss are being thrown
out of the passenger side window
and I begin to laugh.

it's strange how this life
becomes normal so easily.
I am constantly moving,
even while my feet are still.

the purpose in all of this
is to just feel alive.
being comfortable is boring.
staying in one place
is a waste of precious time.

yes, i would rather carry guitar cases
through every club door in this country
than serve another old fashioned
to a bar regular.

i would rather drive 3 hours a night
to share one hotel room

with five passionate human beings
than share a house in philadelphia
that doesn't feel like a home.

i would rather sacrifice sleep
to help others accomplish their dreams
than feel well rested to work a dead end job.

i would rather spend my money
on experiences right now
instead of saving funds
to retire and die.

sometimes i question if this is what I really want.
it comes with sacrifices
and it comes with neglect.
it gets very lonely.

we miss our families
and our friends continue on
living their own lives day by day
with or without us around.

some people say that being a part
of a touring band's crew
is just a way of running from real life,
and that's okay.
i call it an accomplishment.

not many people can run
for seven months straight,
but I sure can.

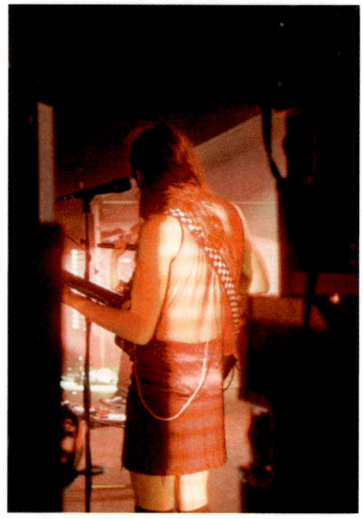

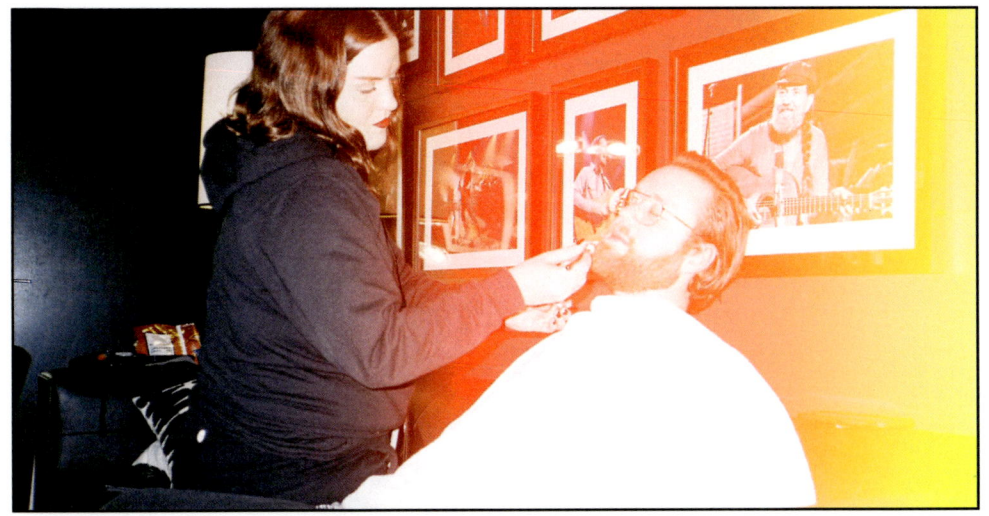

Locations: Germany, Maine, Massachusetts, New Jersey, New York and North Carolina. On tour with: Delain, Hoodie Allen, Kurt Vile and Rainbow Kitten Surprise.

agnostos theos

he showed up at my door unexpected.
the moonlight bounced off of the fresh snow
and onto his face so beautifully.

i am still in disbelief.
the man i only recognize through a screen
is standing in my doorway.

for the past few months
we have been nothing but ships
sailing in the night.
we've both circled this country,
but have never been
in the same place
at the same time;
always one state line away.

but now, here he is,
shivering at my door like a lost puppy.
i welcome him in
with a smile
and a warm hug.
i've been patiently waiting for this moment,
like a kid counting down the days until christmas.

this is my christmas morning.

but see, in my family
there's always something disappointing
about that particular morning.

as a kid, i always expected
to get exactly want i wanted,
but never did.
and I did not get what i wanted
from the man in my doorway.

i wanted to answer questions.
i wanted to laugh.
i wanted to tell stories.
i wanted to be heard.

what i actually got
was a boy too glued
to his phone
to notice me.
a boy too nervous
and too shy
to keep his head held high.

a boy that was more silent than the skies.
a boy who was more interested
in my bed than my brain.
a boy who kept saying he was tired,
you're tired?
i'm tired.

i'm tired of wasting my precious time
on men who wouldn't give me
a second of theirs.
on men who will say anything
to get me into bed.
they will drive all the way
from asbury park
just to get my legs spread.

i'm tired.

a week alone

i just want to be away from humans
but every single job i have
requires me to make small talk with them.

all i want to hear
is the sweet sound of silence
and the chaotic thoughts
coming from my own brain.

instead, i come home after a month
with the sound of a snare drum
stuck in my head.

that's better than facing
the snarling strangers
that feel entitled to ask me
the same vexatious questions
while i serve them drinks
for seven hours straight.

i need a break from the noise.

i just want to lay on my bed and write for hours
with no interruptions from drunk roommates,
and focus on myself without any concern for others.

i love my job
but that does not mean
i was just on vacation.
there's always a little trouble in paradise.

metall pappor

my nights end
in a candle lit tour bus
surrounded by
cheap champagne
and seven strangers.

swedish chatter
has become
my background noise.

i'm having one of those moments.

how did i get here?

i still have moments of gratitude
when i think about how far i've come.

Locations: North Carolina, Pennsylvania, Tennessee and Washington. On tour with Rainbow Kitten Surprise

really high on an 8 hour drive

the concept of heaven and hell
are quite simple to me.

i imagine heaven
to be a home movie on repeat.
a home movie that has captured
every amazing moment in our lives.
we each play the starring role,
and will live in those moments
for all of eternity.
repeat, rewind.
nothing but pure, youthful joy.

i imagine hell
to be a home movie on repeat.
a home movie that has captured
every dark moment in our lives.
distress, humiliation, and sadness.
repeat, rewind.
nothing but black clouds
and endless fear.
a constant headache,
for all of eternity.

boyz night

i can't tell you
that i know what it's like
to fall in love,
because i don't.

what i can tell you
is that meaningful exchange
is what i long for.
i can't seem to find it
in the place i want most.

i find it at 3 am
outside of a tour bus
with people that make
an effort to know me.

maybe i feel this way
because touring forces us
to try,
to talk,
to truly get to know one another.

i really wish i could explain the feeling;
wanting to go home more than anything
and never wanting to see it again.
it's like playing tug of war with myself.
i never know which way to go.
part of me will stand tall
and the other will fall to the ground
no matter what i do.
will this feeling ever change?
do i have to figure it out alone?
because alone is usually all i know
and honestly,
going back to that
terrifies me.

thoughts

listen to the sound
of tires against the wet road,
crickets singing in the distance,
and trees whispering to one another.

this place is quiet.
my thoughts are loud.

embrace it.

i envision these thoughts
pouring out of my skull
like blood from a fresh cut;
scary at first glance
but oddly satisfying.

air them out
in order to heal.

photo by aubrey denis

Lightning Source UK Ltd.
Milton Keynes UK
UKRC010000110620
364748UK00005B/133